Knowledge of SELF

Social Empowerment Learning Framework (S.E.L.F.)

Middle School Edition — Student Workbook

Created by Cedric A. Washington

"Speak it. Believe it. Do it."

Table of Contents

Unit 5: Good People Skills

- • Lesson 1: The Power of Communication
- • Lesson 2: Conflict Is Natural, Respect Is a Choice
- • Lesson 3: Reading the Room
- • Lesson 4: Teamwork Makes the Dream Work
- • Lesson 5: Manners & Respect in the Real World
- • Lesson 6: Helping Hands & Humble Hearts
- • Lesson 7: The SELF-People Skills Check-In

Knowledge of SELF Curriculum — Middle School Student Workbook

Who Lives Like This?! Publishing LLC
www.nerdyouthservices.org

ISBN: 978-1-970680-08-9 (Paperback)

Cover design and interior layout by
Who Lives Like This?! Publishing LLC Design Team

Printed in the United States of America

First Edition — 2025

About the Author

Cedric A. Washington is a master educator, speaker, author, former college basketball player, and the Executive Director of NERD Youth Services, Inc. A native of Gary, Indiana. Over two decades of experience in education, mentoring, and community leadership have fueled his commitment to building culturally responsive, empowering programs for African American youth. As the visionary behind the Knowledge of SELF (Social Empowerment Learning Framework) curriculum, Cedric blends historical awareness, emotional intelligence, leadership training, and personal reflection to cultivate greatness in every student he reaches. His work has been celebrated internationally at education conferences, faith institutions, and youth leadership summits. Cedric's mission is simple but powerful: To equip young people with the self-knowledge, discipline, and purpose they need to transform themselves — and the world.

Daily Affirmations

I AM a trailblazer. I AM destined to succeed. Speak it. Believe it. Do it. – Cedric A. Washington

- I am enough, just as I am.
- My history is powerful, my future is greater.
- I am not what the world calls me—I am who God created me to be.
- I will lead with love, courage, and clarity.
- My skin, my hair, my mind—divinely designed.
- I rise above every label and lie.
- Greatness is not ahead of me; it's within me.
- I walk in wisdom and purpose.
- I am part of a legacy of excellence.
- I build, I uplift, I transform.

Pre-Reflection Survey

Before starting the Knowledge of SELF curriculum, please answer honestly:

1. What do you currently know about your cultural identity?

2. How confident are you in making positive decisions for your future? (1–5)

3. What does success mean to you?

4. Have you ever felt misunderstood in school or in life? Explain.

5. What do you hope to gain from this experience?

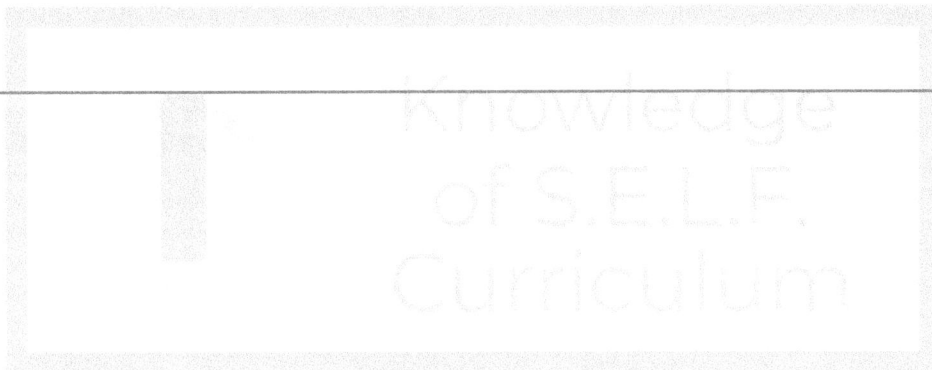

Knowledge of SELF (Social Empowerment Learning Framework)

Middle School Edition — Student Workbook ™

Unit One: SELF Conscience

Lesson 1: Am I a Color? (Part 1)

Objective:
I will learn about the history of the labels placed on African Americans and begin discovering my true identity.

Vocabulary:
- Ethnicity — A group of people who share a common culture, language, or heritage.
- Nationality — The status of belonging to a particular nation by birth or naturalization.

Do Now:
Do you recognize yourself as an African American? What does that mean to you personally?

_____

_____

_____

_____

_____

_____

_____

_____

_____

_____

_____

_____

_____

_____

Mini-Lesson Key Points:
- Terms historically used: Nigger, Negro, Colored, Black, African American, Afro-American.
- Ethnicity vs Nationality.
- True history before slavery.
- Biblical references: Genesis 6–10, Genesis 42:6–8, 23, Exodus 2:19, Deuteronomy 28, Revelation 1:14–15.

Critical Thinking Questions:

1. Do you believe the terms you have been taught truly describe who you are? Why or why not?

_____

_____

_____

_____

_____

_____

_____

_____

_____

_____

_____

_____

_____

2. Why is it important to know your full history — beyond slavery?
[Write two full paragraphs.]

_____

_____

_____

_____

_____

_____

_____

_____

_____

_____

_____

_____

_____

_____

3. How does connecting biblical history to our history empower us?
[Write two full paragraphs.]

_____

_____

_____

_____

_____

_____

_____

_____

_____

_____

_____

Activity: Identity Timeline
Create a simple timeline showing: Pre-slavery identity — Transition into slavery — Modern
identity labels — Your understanding today.

Reflection Journal:
Who are you, beyond a color or label?
[Write two full paragraphs.]

_____
_____
_____
_____
_____
_____
_____
_____
_____
_____
_____
_____
_____
_____

™

Lesson 2: Am I a Color? (Part 2)

Objective:
I will deepen my understanding of my identity and analyze the impact of education, religion, and separation of church and state on historical knowledge.

Vocabulary:
- Curse — A negative consequence placed upon a group of people.
- Slave Trade — The historical forced movement of Africans into slavery across the world.

Do Now:
What is the purpose of going to church? What is the purpose of going to school? Name two things that are similarly done in both.

[Write your answers.]

_____

_____

_____

_____

_____

_____

_____

_____

_____

_____

_____

_____

_____

_____

Mini-Lesson Key Points:
- Deuteronomy Chapter 28 and historical context.
- Atlantic Slave Trade history.
- Separation of historical biblical context from education systems.

Critical Thinking Questions:
1. Why is it powerful to know your history beyond what is taught in school?
[Write two full paragraphs.]

_____
_____
_____
_____
_____
_____
_____
_____
_____
_____
_____
_____
_____
_____

2. How does education influence your sense of identity?
[Write two full paragraphs.]

_____
_____
_____
_____
_____
_____
_____
_____
_____
_____
_____
_____
_____
_____
_____
_____
_____
_____
_____

Activity:
Create a two-column chart comparing what school teaches about African American history vs what biblical history says.

Reflection Journal:
What are you motivated to learn more about after today's lesson?
[Write two full paragraphs.]

_____

_____

_____

_____

_____

_____

_____

_____

_____

_____

_____

_____

_____

_____

_____

_____

_____

_____

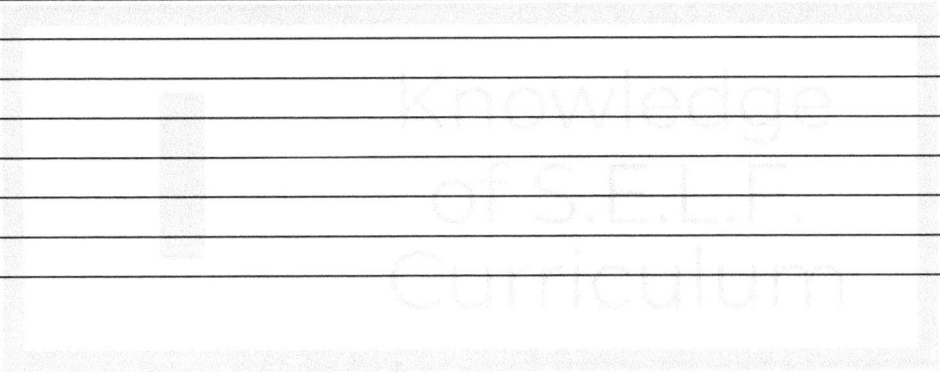

Lesson 3: Love Yourself — The Skin You're In

Objective:
I will learn about melanin, self-love, and embrace my true identity.

Vocabulary:
- Melanin — The pigment responsible for the color of skin, hair, and eyes.

Do Now:
Have you ever heard someone say, "I don't want to get too dark"? What does that statement mean to you?
[Write your reflection.]

_____

_____

_____

_____

_____

_____

_____

_____

_____

_____

_____

_____

_____

Mini-Lesson Key Points:
- Melanin's power and significance (6 protons, 6 neutrons, 6 electrons = 666 myth).
- Skin tone pride through the Skin Tone Chart.
- Positive vs negative language: "black" vs "brown."

Critical Thinking Questions:

1. How does understanding melanin empower your identity?
[Write two full paragraphs.]

_____

_____

_____

_____

_____

_____

_____

_____

_____

_____

_____

_____

_____

_____

_____

_____

_____

2. Why is language important when talking about identity?
[Write two full paragraphs.]

_____

_____

_____

_____

_____

_____

_____

_____

_____

_____

_____

_____

_____

_____

_____

_____

Activity:

Skin Tone Matching — Match your complexion on the Skin Tone Chart and reflect on how you feel about your beautiful shade of brown.

Color Me Human | Skin Tone Chart

Reflection Journal:
How will you celebrate your true self starting today?

_____
_____
_____
_____
_____
_____
_____
_____
_____
_____
_____
_____
_____
_____
_____
_____
_____
_____
_____
_____

Lesson 4: Attributes/Characteristics of SELF

Objective:

I will reflect on my personal traits, emotions, values, and how they form my SELF identity.

Vocabulary:

- Attributes — Qualities or features regarded as a characteristic of someone.
- Characteristics — Distinguishing traits or qualities.

Do Now:

What are three qualities you admire most in yourself?

_____

_____

_____

_____

Mini-Lesson Key Points:

- Knowing your strengths and areas for growth empowers your journey.
- Reflection creates clarity.

Critical Thinking Questions:

1. What are your greatest strengths and how do they help you?
[Write two full paragraphs.]

_____

_____

_____

_____

_____

_____

_____

_____

_____

_____

_____

_____

_____

_____

_____

_____

_____

_____

_____

2. What is one quality you would like to improve about yourself?
[Write two full paragraphs.]

_____

_____

_____

_____

_____

_____

_____

_____

_____

_____

TM

_____

Activity:
Personal Attribute Chart — List 5 strengths and 2 areas for growth.

Reflection Journal:
Who are you today, and who are you becoming?
[Write two full paragraphs.]

_____
_____
_____
_____
_____
_____
_____
_____
_____
_____
_____
_____
_____
_____
_____
_____
_____
_____
_____
_____
_____
_____
_____
_____
_____

Lesson 5: Ethics

Objective:
I will explore my personal ethics and understand how they shape my decisions.

Vocabulary:
- Ethics — Moral principles that govern a person's behavior or conducting of an activity.

Do Now:
Name three values that are most important to you.

_____
_____
_____
_____
_____
_____
_____
_____
_____
_____

Mini-Lesson Key Points:
- Ethics determine choices.
- Values drive behavior.

Critical Thinking Questions:
1. Why is it important to have strong personal ethics?
[Write two full paragraphs.]

_____
_____
_____
_____
_____
_____
_____
_____
_____
_____
_____
_____
_____
_____

2. How do ethics influence how you treat others?
[Write two full paragraphs.]

_____

_____

_____

_____

_____

_____

_____

_____

_____

_____

_____

Activity:
Top Ten Values List — Write the 10 values you live by.

Reflection Journal:
What value will you never compromise?
[Write two full paragraphs.]

_____
_____
_____
_____
_____
_____
_____
_____
_____
_____
_____
_____
_____
_____
_____
_____
_____
_____
_____
_____
_____
_____
_____
_____
_____

Lesson 6: Image

Objective:
I will examine how my self-image and public image are shaped and how to live authentically.

Vocabulary:
- Authenticity — Being true to one's own personality, spirit, or character.

Do Now:
How do you think people view you? How do you want them to view you?

_____
_____
_____
_____
_____
_____
_____
_____
_____
_____
_____

Mini-Lesson Key Points:
- Private vs public self.
- Authenticity vs pleasing others.

Critical Thinking Questions:
1. What makes it hard to be your true self sometimes?
[Write two full paragraphs.]

_____
_____
_____
_____
_____
_____
_____
_____

_____

_____

_____

_____

_____

_____

_____

_____

_____

_____

2. How can you live more authentically every day?
[Write two full paragraphs.]

_____

_____

_____

_____

_____

_____

_____

_____

_____

_____

_____

_____

_____

_____

_____

_____

Activity:
Public vs Private Self Mapping — Write traits you show publicly vs privately.

Reflection Journal:
What is the legacy of the "real you"?
[Write two full paragraphs.]

_____

_____

_____

_____

_____

_____

_____

_____

_____

_____

_____

_____

_____

_____

_____

_____

_____

_____

_____

_____

_____

_____

_____

Lesson 7: Achievements

Objective:
I will celebrate my achievements and set new personal goals.

Vocabulary:
- Achievement — A thing done successfully with effort, skill, or courage.

Do Now:
What is one accomplishment you are proud of?

_____
_____
_____
_____
_____
_____
_____
_____
_____
_____
_____
_____

Mini-Lesson Key Points:
- Achievements are proof of growth.
- Small wins build big dreams.

Critical Thinking Questions:
1. How do your achievements show who you are?
[Write two full paragraphs.]

_____
_____
_____
_____
_____
_____
_____
_____
_____
_____
_____
_____
_____

2. What is a new achievement you want to earn this year?
[Write two full paragraphs.]

_____
_____
_____
_____
_____
_____
_____
_____
_____
_____
_____

Activity:
Award Letter — Write yourself an award letter for your proudest accomplishment.

Reflection Journal:
What achievement will your future self-thank you for?
[Write two full paragraphs.]

_____

_____

_____

_____

_____

_____

_____

_____

_____

_____

_____

_____

_____

_____

_____

_____

Knowledge of SELF (Social Empowerment Learning Framework)

Middle School Edition — Student Workbook ™

Unit Two: SELF Governing

Lesson 1: Health and Nutrition

Objective:
I will learn how health and nutrition affect my focus, energy, emotions, and success.

Vocabulary:
- Nutrition — The process of providing or obtaining the food necessary for health and growth.
- Health — The state of being free from illness or injury.

Do Now:
What is your favorite healthy food or snack? Why?

_____
_____
_____
_____
_____
_____
_____
_____
_____
_____
_____

Mini-Lesson Key Points:
- Your body is your temple.
- Foods like sea moss, fruits, vegetables, and hydration fuel greatness.

Critical Thinking Questions:
1. How does eating healthy improve your ability to succeed?
[Write two full paragraphs.]

_____
_____
_____
_____
_____
_____
_____
_____
_____
_____

2. What are small daily habits that could improve your overall health?
[Write two full paragraphs.]

_____
_____
_____
_____
_____
_____
_____
_____
_____
_____
_____
_____
_____
_____

Activity:
Create Your Healthy Lifestyle Plan — Name 3 healthy habits you will practice this month.

Reflection Journal:

How will you treat your body with more respect after today?

[Write two full paragraphs.]

_____

_____

_____

_____

_____

_____

_____

_____

_____

_____

_____

_____

_____

_____

_____

_____

_____

_____

_____

_____

_____

_____

_____

_____

_____

_____

_____

_____

_____

_____

_____

_____

_____

_____

Lesson 2: The Importance of FOCUS

Objective:
I will understand and apply the FOCUS method (Fallback, Opportunities, Cultivate, Understanding, Succeed) to my dreams.

Vocabulary:
- Focus — Directed attention toward a goal or objective.

Do Now:
Describe a time you lost focus. What happened?

_____
_____
_____
_____
_____
_____
_____
_____
_____
_____

Mini-Lesson Key Points:
- **Fallback**: Separate yourself from distractions.
- **Opportunities**: Seek alignments with people and resources that support your vision.
- **Cultivate**: Practice and build your skills.
- **Understanding**: Accept that everyone won't understand your grind.
- **Succeed**: Celebrate each victory along the way.

Critical Thinking Questions:
1. What is one area of your life where you need more focus?
[Write two full paragraphs.]

_____
_____
_____
_____
_____
_____
_____
_____
_____
_____

2. Why is it important to protect your focus and energy?
[Write two full paragraphs.]

_____

_____

_____

_____

_____

_____

_____

_____

_____

_____

_____

Activity:

Focus Goal Sheet — Write down a goal and apply the FOCUS method to reach it.

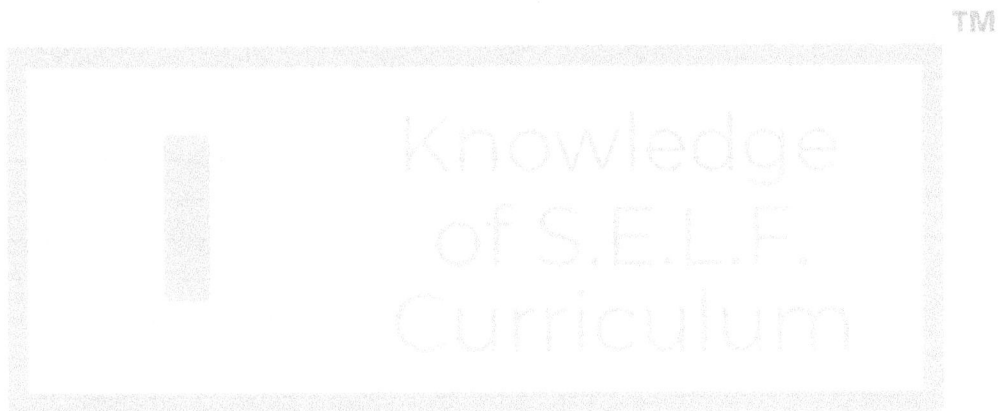

Reflection Journal:
How will focusing change your future?
[Write two full paragraphs.]

_____
_____
_____
_____
_____
_____
_____
_____
_____
_____
_____
_____
_____
_____
_____
_____
_____
_____
_____
_____
_____
_____
_____
_____
_____
_____
_____
_____

Lesson 3: Role Modeling

Objective:
I will understand the impact of role modeling and how my actions influence others.

Vocabulary:
- Role Model — A person looked to by others as an example to be imitated.

Do Now:
Name someone you look up to and what you admire about them.

_____
_____
_____
_____
_____
_____
_____
_____

Mini-Lesson Key Points:
- Leadership starts by example.
- Someone is always watching and learning from you.

Critical Thinking Questions:
1. What qualities make someone a powerful role model?
[Write two full paragraphs.]

_____
_____
_____
_____
_____
_____
_____
_____
_____
_____
_____
_____
_____
_____
_____
_____

2. What kind of role model do you want to be?
[Write two full paragraphs.]

_____

_____

_____

_____

_____

_____

_____

_____

_____

_____

Activity:

Role Model Reflection — Identify 3 ways you can be a positive influence in your community starting today.

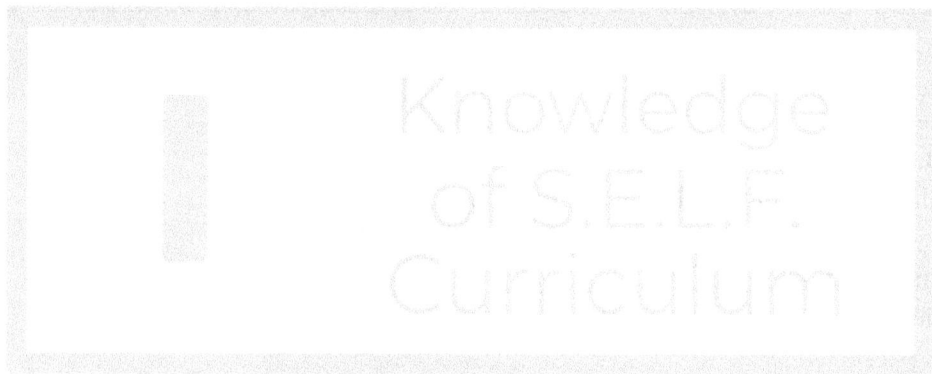

Reflection Journal:

Describe the legacy you want to leave through your example.

[Write two full paragraphs.]

_____
_____
_____
_____
_____
_____
_____
_____
_____
_____
_____
_____
_____
_____
_____
_____
_____
_____
_____
_____
_____
_____
_____
_____
_____
_____
_____
_____

Lesson 4: Hygiene

Objective:
I will learn how daily hygiene habits affect my health, self-esteem, and opportunities.

Vocabulary:
- Hygiene — Conditions or practices conducive to maintaining health and preventing disease.

Do Now:
Why do you think first impressions are important?

_____
_____
_____
_____
_____
_____
_____
_____
_____
_____

Mini-Lesson Key Points:
- Good hygiene builds confidence.
- Hygiene shows self-respect and care for others.

Critical Thinking Questions:
1. How does personal hygiene affect how you feel about yourself?
[Write two full paragraphs.]

_____
_____
_____
_____
_____
_____
_____
_____
_____

2. How can good hygiene help you succeed in school, sports, or life?
[Write two full paragraphs.]

_____
_____
_____
_____
_____
_____
_____
_____
_____
_____
_____
_____

Activity:
Daily Hygiene Checklist — Create a checklist of your daily hygiene habits.

Reflection Journal:
What hygiene habit will you improve starting today?
[Write two full paragraphs.]

_____
_____
_____
_____
_____
_____
_____
_____
_____
_____
_____
_____
_____
_____
_____
_____
_____
_____
_____
_____
_____
_____
_____
_____
_____
_____
_____
_____
_____

Lesson 5: Emotional Maturity

Objective:
I will understand how controlling my emotions shows strength and leadership.

Vocabulary:
- Maturity — The ability to respond to situations with wisdom, patience, and self-control.

Do Now:
Describe a time when you had to stay calm even though you were upset.

_____
_____
_____
_____
_____
_____
_____
_____
_____
_____
_____

Mini-Lesson Key Points:
- Emotional maturity is managing emotions, not letting them manage you.
- Growth is seen when you respond, not react.

Critical Thinking Questions:
1. Why is emotional maturity important in leadership?
[Write two full paragraphs.]

_____
_____
_____
_____
_____
_____
_____
_____
_____
_____
_____

2. What helps you stay calm in difficult situations?
[Write two full paragraphs.]

_____
_____
_____
_____
_____
_____
_____
_____
_____
_____
_____
_____

Activity:
Emotional Response Plan — Write 3 strategies you can use when feeling angry, sad, or frustrated.

Reflection Journal:

How will emotional maturity strengthen your future relationships and success?

[Write two full paragraphs.]

_____

_____

_____

_____

_____

_____

_____

_____

_____

_____

_____

_____

_____

_____

_____

_____

_____

_____

_____

_____

_____

_____

_____

_____

_____

_____

_____

_____

_____

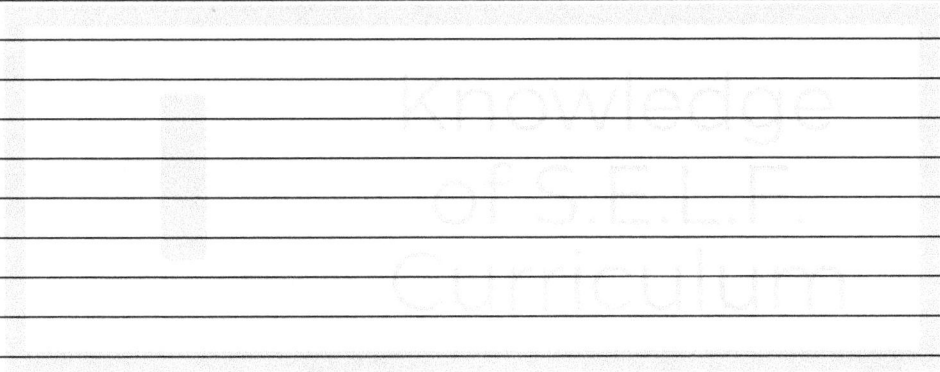

Lesson 6: Puberty

Objective:
I will understand the physical, emotional, and social changes during puberty.

Vocabulary:
- Puberty — The period of life when a person becomes capable of reproduction.

Do Now:
What question do you have about growing up?

_____
_____
_____
_____
_____
_____
_____
_____
_____
_____
_____
_____
_____
_____
_____

Mini-Lesson Key Points:
- Body changes are normal.
- Puberty also brings emotional and mental growth.

Critical Thinking Questions:
1. How can understanding puberty help you better manage change?
[Write two full paragraphs.]

_____
_____
_____
_____
_____
_____
_____
_____
_____
_____

2. Why is it important to talk openly about growing up?
[Write two full paragraphs.]

_____
_____
_____
_____
_____
_____
_____
_____
_____
_____
_____
_____

Activity:
Puberty Myths vs Facts — Write one myth and the real fact about puberty.

Reflection Journal:
What new information about puberty did you learn today?
[Write two full paragraphs.]

_____
_____
_____
_____
_____
_____
_____
_____
_____
_____
_____
_____
_____
_____
_____
_____
_____
_____
_____
_____
_____
_____
_____
_____
_____
_____
_____
_____
_____
_____

Lesson 7: Peer Pressure

Objective:
I will recognize peer pressure and practice standing strong in my values.

Vocabulary:
- Peer Pressure — Influence from members of one's peer group.

Do Now:
Have you ever felt pressured by friends? How did you respond?

_____
_____
_____
_____
_____
_____
_____
_____
_____
_____
_____
_____
_____
_____

Mini-Lesson Key Points:
- Peer pressure can be positive or negative.
- Learning to say "NO" protects your goals.

Critical Thinking Questions:
1. What is an example of positive peer pressure?
[Write two full paragraphs.]

_____
_____
_____
_____
_____
_____
_____
_____
_____
_____
_____

2. How can you stand strong when others are trying to lead you the wrong way?
[Write two full paragraphs.]

_____

_____

_____

_____

_____

_____

_____

_____

_____

_____

_____

_____

_____

_____

Activity:
Peer Pressure Defense Strategies — Write down 3 ways to resist negative peer pressure.

Reflection Journal:
Describe a situation where you stayed true to yourself even when it was hard.
[Write two full paragraphs.]

_____
_____
_____
_____
_____
_____
_____
_____
_____
_____
_____
_____
_____
_____
_____
_____
_____
_____
_____
_____
_____
_____
_____
_____
_____
_____
_____
_____
_____
_____
_____

Knowledge of SELF (Social Empowerment Learning Framework)

Middle School Edition — Student Workbook

Unit Three: Social Conscience

Lesson 1: How to Be Effective in Your Community

Objective:
I will learn how to be an agent of positive change in my community.

Vocabulary:
- Community — A group of people living in the same place or having characteristics in common.

Do Now:
What is one change you would like to see in your neighborhood?

_____

_____

_____

_____

_____

_____

_____

_____

_____

_____

_____

_____

_____

_____

_____

Mini-Lesson Key Points:
- Community starts with caring.
- Small actions = Big changes over time.

Critical Thinking Questions:
1. How can young people make a difference in their community?
[Write two full paragraphs.]

_____

_____

_____

_____

_____

_____

_____

_____

_____

_____

_____

_____

_____

_____

_____

2. What are ways you can start giving back today?
[Write two full paragraphs.]

_____

_____

_____

_____

_____

_____

_____

_____

_____

_____

_____

_____

_____

_____

Activity:
My First Community Action Plan — Write 3 things you could do to make your community better.

Reflection Journal:
How do you want your community to remember your contribution?
[Write two full paragraphs.]

_____
_____
_____
_____
_____
_____
_____
_____
_____
_____
_____
_____
_____
_____
_____
_____
_____
_____
_____
_____
_____
_____
_____
_____
_____
_____
_____
_____
_____
_____
_____
_____
_____
_____
_____

Lesson 2: African American Leaders

Objective:
I will explore powerful African American leaders and understand the traits of leadership.

Vocabulary:
- Leadership — The action of leading a group of people or an organization.

Do Now:
Name a Black leader who inspires you. Why?

_____
_____
_____
_____
_____
_____
_____
_____
_____
_____
_____
_____
_____
_____
_____

Mini-Lesson Key Points:
- Leadership is about service, courage, and vision.
- Every great leader started with a dream and a cause.

Critical Thinking Questions:
1. What leadership qualities do you admire most?
[Write two full paragraphs.]

_____
_____
_____
_____
_____
_____
_____
_____
_____
_____

2. How can you develop leadership skills starting today?
[Write two full paragraphs.]

_____
_____
_____
_____
_____
_____
_____
_____
_____
_____
_____
_____
_____
_____

Activity:
My Leadership Legacy — Write down 5 leadership traits you want to be known for.

Reflection Journal:
Who will you inspire through your leadership?
[Write two full paragraphs.]

_____
_____
_____
_____
_____
_____
_____
_____
_____
_____
_____
_____
_____
_____
_____
_____
_____
_____
_____
_____
_____
_____
_____
_____
_____
_____
_____
_____

Lesson 3: Hip Hop: The Culture

Objective:
I will explore the cultural power of Hip Hop and how it shapes identity, activism, and empowerment.

Vocabulary:
- Culture — The ideas, customs, and social behaviors of a particular people or society.

Do Now:
What does Hip Hop mean to you personally?

_____
_____
_____
_____
_____
_____
_____
_____
_____
_____
_____
_____
_____
_____

Mini-Lesson Key Points:
- Hip Hop is a voice for the voiceless.
- Hip Hop tells our stories, struggles, and dreams.

Critical Thinking Questions:
1. How has Hip Hop been a tool for change?
[Write two full paragraphs.]

_____
_____
_____
_____
_____
_____
_____
_____
_____

2. How can music inspire people to fight for justice and unity?
[Write two full paragraphs.]

_____
_____
_____
_____
_____
_____
_____
_____
_____
_____
_____
_____
_____
_____

Activity:
Create Your Empowerment Verse — Write a short rap or spoken word piece that uplifts, inspires, or speaks truth.

Reflection Journal:
What message would you want to share with the world through your art?
[Write two full paragraphs.]

_____
_____
_____
_____
_____
_____
_____
_____
_____
_____
_____
_____
_____
_____
_____
_____
_____
_____
_____
_____
_____
_____
_____
_____
_____
_____
_____
_____
_____
_____
_____

Lesson 4: Family Dynamics

Objective:
I will explore how family influences identity, values, and my role in the world.

Vocabulary:
- Dynamics — Forces or properties that stimulate growth, development, or change.

Do Now:
Describe one lesson you have learned from your family.

_____
_____
_____
_____
_____
_____
_____
_____
_____
_____
_____
_____
_____

Mini-Lesson Key Points:
- Family is your first teacher.
- Family shapes your emotional, social, and cultural blueprint.

Critical Thinking Questions:
1. How has your family influenced your dreams and goals?
[Write two full paragraphs.]

_____
_____
_____
_____
_____
_____
_____
_____
_____
_____

2. What values from your family do you want to carry forward?
[Write two full paragraphs.]

_____
_____
_____
_____
_____
_____
_____
_____
_____
_____
_____
_____
_____
_____
_____
_____

Activity:
Family Values Tree — Draw a tree and on each branch, write a positive value or lesson you learned from family.

Reflection Journal:
What legacy do you want to build starting from the roots your family gave you?
[Write two full paragraphs.]

_____
_____
_____
_____
_____
_____
_____
_____
_____
_____
_____
_____
_____
_____
_____
_____
_____
_____
_____
_____
_____
_____
_____
_____
_____
_____
_____
_____
_____
_____
_____
_____
_____
_____
_____
_____
_____

Lesson 5: Accountability

Objective:

I will learn how taking ownership of my actions builds power, trust, and respect.

Vocabulary:

- Accountability — Taking responsibility for one's actions and decisions.

Do Now:

When was a time you had to own up to something you did?

_____
_____
_____
_____
_____
_____
_____
_____
_____
_____
_____
_____
_____
_____
_____
_____

Mini-Lesson Key Points:

- Leaders don't make excuses.
- True power comes from ownership, not blame.

Critical Thinking Questions:

1. Why is it important to hold yourself accountable?

[Write two full paragraphs.]

_____
_____
_____
_____
_____
_____
_____
_____
_____
_____
_____

2. How does accountability strengthen relationships?
[Write two full paragraphs.]

_____

_____

_____

_____

_____

_____

_____

_____

_____

_____

_____

_____

_____

_____

Activity:
Accountability Commitment — Write one action you will take responsibility for this week.

Reflection Journal:

How can you become a stronger leader by practicing accountability?

[Write two full paragraphs.]

_____

_____

_____

_____

_____

_____

_____

_____

_____

_____

_____

_____

_____

_____

_____

_____

_____

_____

_____

_____

_____

_____

Lesson 6: Community Service and Giving Back

Objective:
I will understand the importance of serving others to uplift my community and my spirit.

Vocabulary:
- Service — The action of helping or doing work for others.

Do Now:
What is one act of kindness you have given or received recently?

_____
_____
_____
_____
_____
_____
_____
_____
_____
_____
_____
_____
_____
_____

Mini-Lesson Key Points:
- Service strengthens communities and hearts.
- Giving back multiplies blessings.

Critical Thinking Questions:
1. How does helping others make you stronger?
[Write two full paragraphs.]

_____
_____
_____
_____
_____
_____
_____
_____

2. What gifts and talents can you use to help others?
[Write two full paragraphs.]

_____
_____
_____
_____
_____
_____
_____
_____
_____
_____
_____
_____
_____
_____
_____
_____
_____

Activity:
Service Project Plan — Brainstorm a small project you could do to give back to your school, neighborhood, or family.

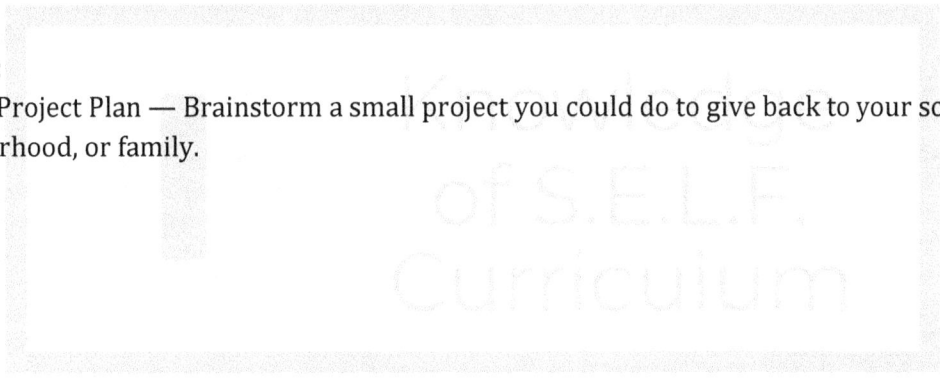

Reflection Journal:
Why is it important for young leaders to serve?
[Write two full paragraphs.]

_____

_____

_____

_____

_____

_____

_____

_____

_____

_____

_____

_____

_____

_____

_____

_____

_____

_____

_____

_____

_____

_____

_____

_____

_____

_____

_____

_____

Lesson 7: Building Your Legacy

Objective:
I will create a vision for the impact I want to leave on my family, community, and world.

Vocabulary:
- Legacy — Something handed down from one generation to the next.

Do Now:
When people speak about you in the future, what do you want them to say?

_____

_____

_____

_____

_____

_____

_____

_____

_____

_____

_____

_____

_____

_____

Mini-Lesson Key Points:
- Every action plants a seed for your legacy.
- You write your story every day.

Critical Thinking Questions:
1. What legacy do you want to leave behind?
[Write two full paragraphs.]

_____

_____

_____

_____

_____

_____

_____

_____

_____

_____

_____

2. What steps can you take today to build that legacy?
[Write two full paragraphs.]

_____
_____
_____
_____
_____
_____
_____
_____
_____
_____
_____
_____
_____
_____
_____
_____

Activity:
Legacy Vision Statement — Write your personal mission statement for the life you want to live.

Reflection Journal:
How will you use your gifts to uplift others?
[Write two full paragraphs.]

_____
_____
_____
_____
_____
_____
_____
_____
_____
_____
_____
_____

_____
_____
_____
_____
_____
_____
_____
_____
_____
_____
_____
_____
_____
_____
_____
_____
_____
_____

Knowledge of SELF (Social Empowerment Learning Framework)

™

Middle School Edition — Student Workbook

Unit Four: Aspirations

Lesson 1: What I Want to Be When I Grow Up

Objective:
I will dream boldly about my future and connect my passions to possible career paths.

Vocabulary:
- Aspiration — A hope or ambition of achieving something.

Do Now:
What is one career you would love to have? Why?

_____
_____
_____
_____
_____
_____
_____
_____
_____
_____
_____

Mini-Lesson Key Points:
- Dreams start with imagination but grow through planning.
- Your future begins with your focus today.

Critical Thinking Questions:
1. What are your biggest dreams for your future?
[Write two full paragraphs.]

_____
_____
_____
_____
_____
_____

2. How can your talents and passions lead you toward your dreams?
[Write two full paragraphs.]

_____

_____

_____

_____

_____

_____

_____

_____

_____

_____

_____

_____

_____

_____

_____

_____

Activity:
Dream Career Web — Create a mind map connecting your interests to possible careers.

Reflection Journal:
Describe a day in the life of your dream career.
[Write two full paragraphs.]

_____
_____
_____
_____
_____
_____
_____
_____
_____
_____
_____
_____

_____
_____
_____
_____
_____
_____
_____
_____
_____
_____
_____
_____
_____
_____

Lesson 2: Career Day Panel Preparation and Event

Objective:
I will prepare to interact professionally with career mentors and expand my view of career possibilities.

Vocabulary:
- Networking — The action of interacting with others to exchange information and develop contacts.

Do Now:
If you could ask a professional one question about their career, what would you ask?

_____
_____
_____
_____
_____
_____
_____
_____
_____
_____
_____
_____

Mini-Lesson Key Points:
- Preparation creates opportunity.
- Every conversation can be a bridge to your dreams.

Critical Thinking Questions:
1. Why is it important to network with people doing what you dream of?
[Write two full paragraphs.]

_____
_____
_____
_____
_____
_____
_____
_____

2. What can you learn from hearing about someone else's career journey?
[Write two full paragraphs.]

_____
_____
_____
_____
_____
_____
_____
_____
_____
_____
_____
_____
_____
_____

Activity:
Career Day Question List — Write 5 questions you would ask a professional about their career journey.

Reflection Journal:
What was the most inspiring thing you learned from Career Day?
[Write two full paragraphs.]

_____
_____
_____
_____
_____
_____
_____
_____
_____
_____
_____
_____
_____
_____
_____
_____
_____
_____
_____
_____
_____
_____
_____
_____
_____
_____
_____
_____
_____

Lesson 3: Resume Workshop

Objective:
I will learn the basics of resume writing and begin building my personal resume.

Vocabulary:
- Resume — A document listing your skills, education, and experience.

Do Now:
What are three skills or accomplishments you would include on a resume?

_____
_____
_____
_____
_____
_____
_____
_____
_____
_____
_____
_____
_____
_____
_____

Mini-Lesson Key Points:
- Your resume speaks for you before you enter the room.
- Start documenting your leadership, skills, and hard work early.

Critical Thinking Questions:
1. Why is it important to start building your resume now?
[Write two full paragraphs.]

_____
_____
_____
_____
_____
_____
_____
_____
_____
_____

2. How can you build skills and experiences to strengthen your resume?
[Write two full paragraphs.]

_____

_____

_____

_____

_____

_____

_____

_____

_____

_____

_____

_____

_____

_____

_____

Activity:
Build Your First Resume — Start listing your activities, skills, awards, and leadership roles.

Reflection Journal:
What is one accomplishment you are most proud to include on your resume?
[Write two full paragraphs.]

_____
_____
_____
_____
_____
_____
_____
_____
_____
_____
_____
_____
_____
_____
_____
_____
_____
_____
_____
_____
_____
_____
_____
_____
_____
_____
_____
_____
_____
_____
_____
_____
_____
_____

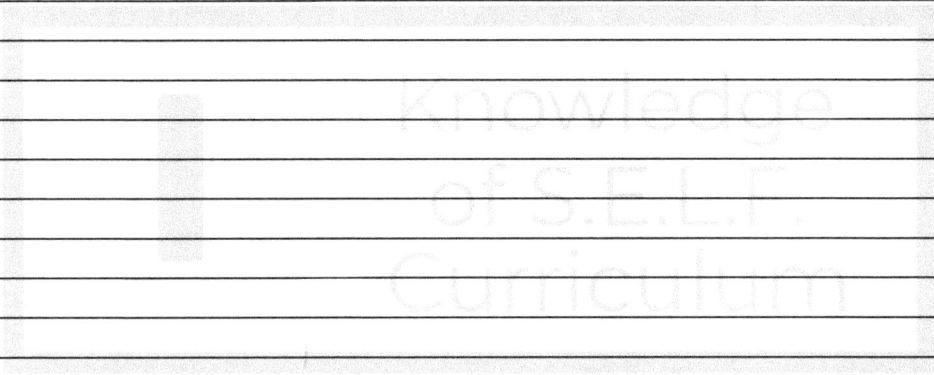

Lesson 4: Short Term Goals

Objective:
I will set clear and achievable short-term goals that build momentum toward my dreams.

Vocabulary:
- Goal — The object of a person's ambition or effort; an aim or desired result.

Do Now:
What is one goal you could accomplish in the next 30 days?

_____
_____
_____
_____
_____
_____
_____
_____
_____
_____
_____
_____
_____
_____

Mini-Lesson Key Points:
- Big dreams require small, focused steps.
- Success builds by stacking short-term wins.

Critical Thinking Questions:
1. Why is it important to set short-term goals?
[Write two full paragraphs.]

_____
_____
_____
_____
_____
_____
_____
_____
_____
_____

2. How do small victories lead to bigger successes?
[Write two full paragraphs.]

_____

_____

_____

_____

_____

_____

_____

_____

_____

_____

_____

_____

_____

_____

Activity:
Goal Setting Sheet — List three short-term goals and steps to achieve them.

Reflection Journal:
What will you feel like when you achieve your next short-term goal?
[Write two full paragraphs.]

_____
_____
_____
_____
_____
_____
_____
_____
_____
_____
_____
_____
_____
_____
_____
_____
_____
_____
_____
_____
_____
_____
_____
_____
_____
_____
_____
_____
_____
_____
_____
_____

Lesson 5: Long Term Goals

Objective:
I will plan and dream boldly about long-term goals and life achievements.

Vocabulary:
- Vision — The ability to think about or plan the future with imagination or wisdom.

Do Now:
Where do you see yourself in 10 years?

_____
_____
_____
_____
_____
_____
_____
_____
_____
_____
_____
_____
_____
_____

Mini-Lesson Key Points:
- Vision creates direction.
- Planning prevents drifting.

Critical Thinking Questions:
1. What are three dreams you have for your future?
[Write two full paragraphs.]

_____
_____
_____
_____
_____
_____
_____
_____
_____
_____

2. Why is it important to dream big but stay patient?
[Write two full paragraphs.]

_____
_____
_____
_____
_____
_____
_____
_____
_____
_____
_____
_____
_____
_____

_____

Activity:
Life Blueprint — Draw a path from your current age to your dream future.

Reflection Journal:
What will you need to start doing today to reach your long-term goals?
[Write two full paragraphs.]

_____
_____
_____
_____
_____
_____
_____
_____
_____
_____
_____
_____
_____
_____
_____
_____
_____
_____
_____
_____
_____
_____
_____
_____
_____
_____
_____

Lesson 6: Financial Literacy

Objective:
I will understand the basics of managing money, saving, and making smart financial decisions.

Vocabulary:
- Budget — A plan for making and spending money.

Do Now:
If you earned $50 today, how would you spend or save it?

_____

Mini-Lesson Key Points:
- Smart money habits build freedom.
- Financial discipline beats financial struggle.

Critical Thinking Questions:
1. Why is it important to manage money wisely even at a young age?
[Write two full paragraphs.]

_____

2. How can financial literacy help you reach your goals faster?
[Write two full paragraphs.]

_____

Activity:
Simple Budget Plan — Create a basic budget for saving and spending $100.

Reflection Journal:
How will you become a wise money manager?
[Write two full paragraphs.]

_____
_____
_____
_____
_____
_____
_____
_____
_____
_____
_____
_____
_____
_____
_____
_____
_____
_____
_____
_____

Lesson 7: Building Wealth and Generational Legacy

Objective:
I will learn the importance of building wealth and leaving a positive legacy for future generations.

Vocabulary:
- Asset — Anything valuable that is owned.

Do Now:
What does "generational wealth" mean to you?

_____
_____
_____
_____
_____
_____
_____
_____
_____
_____
_____
_____
_____
_____

Mini-Lesson Key Points:
- True success is building for the next generation.
- Ownership is power.

Critical Thinking Questions:
1. Why is it important to think about building wealth early?
[Write two full paragraphs.]

_____
_____
_____
_____
_____
_____
_____
_____
_____
_____

2. How can you use your talents and knowledge to create a legacy?
[Write two full paragraphs.]

_____
_____
_____
_____
_____
_____
_____
_____
_____
_____
_____
_____
_____
_____
_____

™

Activity:
Legacy Plan — Write three ways you can build and pass on wealth starting now.

Reflection Journal:
What legacy do you want your future family to inherit from you?
[Write two full paragraphs.]

_____

_____

_____

_____

_____

_____

_____

_____

_____

_____

_____

_____

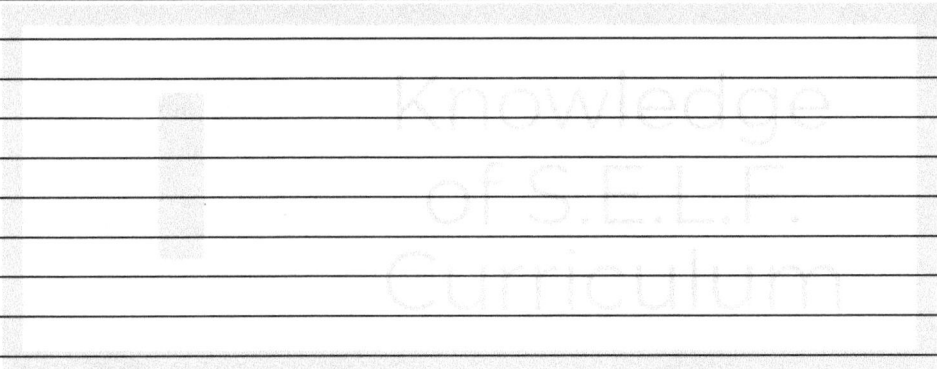

_____

_____

_____

_____

_____

_____

_____

_____

_____

_____

Knowledge of SELF (Social Empowerment Learning Framework)

Middle School Edition — Student Workbook ™

Unit Five: Good People Skills

Lesson 1: Conflict Resolution

Objective:
I will learn how to handle conflicts in peaceful, mature, and effective ways.

Vocabulary:
- Resolution — The action of solving a problem or dispute.

Do Now:
Describe a conflict you had with someone. How was it resolved?

_____
_____
_____
_____
_____
_____
_____
_____
_____
_____
_____
_____
_____
_____

Mini-Lesson Key Points:
- Conflict is normal; peaceful resolution is powerful.
- Listening, empathy, and patience are keys.

Critical Thinking Questions:
1. Why is peaceful conflict resolution important for leadership and relationships?
[Write two full paragraphs.]

_____
_____
_____
_____
_____
_____
_____
_____
_____
_____

2. What strategies can you use when disagreements arise?
[Write two full paragraphs.]

_____

_____

_____

_____

_____

_____

_____

_____

_____

_____

_____

_____

_____

_____

_____

Activity:
Conflict Role Play — Practice resolving a disagreement respectfully and calmly.

Reflection Journal:
How will you handle conflict differently moving forward?
[Write two full paragraphs.]

_____
_____
_____
_____
_____
_____
_____
_____
_____
_____
_____
_____
_____
_____
_____
_____
_____
_____
_____
_____
_____
_____
_____

Lesson 2: Group Cooperation

Objective:
I will build the skills needed to work well with others and thrive in group environments.

Vocabulary:
- Cooperation — Working together toward a common goal.

Do Now:
What is the best team you have ever been a part of? Why did it work?

_____
_____
_____
_____
_____
_____
_____
_____
_____
_____
_____
_____
_____

Mini-Lesson Key Points:
- Every great movement was built through teamwork.
- Trust, communication, and respect are keys.

Critical Thinking Questions:
1. How do great teams overcome differences and succeed?
[Write two full paragraphs.]

_____
_____
_____
_____
_____
_____
_____
_____
_____
_____
_____

2. How can you contribute to a positive team environment?
[Write two full paragraphs.]

_____

_____

_____

_____

_____

_____

_____

_____

_____

_____

_____

_____

_____

_____

_____

Activity:
Team Challenge — Collaborate with a group to solve a creative task together.

Reflection Journal:
What strengths do you bring to a team?
[Write two full paragraphs.]

_____

_____

_____

_____

_____

_____

_____

_____

_____

_____

_____

_____

_____

_____

_____

_____

_____

_____

_____

_____

_____

_____

_____

_____

Lesson 3: Friendship

Objective:
I will learn how to build and nurture meaningful, healthy friendships.

Vocabulary:
- Loyalty — A strong feeling of support or allegiance.

Do Now:
Name three qualities that make a great friend.

_____
_____
_____
_____
_____
_____
_____
_____
_____
_____
_____
_____
_____
_____

Mini-Lesson Key Points:
- True friendships uplift and inspire.
- Healthy boundaries and support are essential.

Critical Thinking Questions:
1. What makes a friendship strong and lasting?
[Write two full paragraphs.]

_____
_____
_____
_____
_____
_____
_____
_____
_____
_____

2. How can you be the type of friend you want to have?
[Write two full paragraphs.]

_____
_____
_____
_____
_____
_____
_____
_____
_____
_____
_____
_____
_____

TM

Activity:
Friendship Vision Statement — Write a description of your ideal friendship circle.

Reflection Journal:
How will you show up differently in your friendships moving forward?
[Write two full paragraphs.]

_____

_____

_____

_____

_____

_____

_____

_____

_____

_____

_____

_____

_____

_____

_____

_____

_____

_____

_____

_____

_____

_____

_____

_____

Lesson 4: Identifying Unhealthy Relationships

Objective:
I will learn the signs of unhealthy friendships and relationships and how to protect my peace.

Vocabulary:
- Boundaries — Guidelines that define how others can treat you.

Do Now:
Have you ever had a friendship or relationship that didn't feel right? What happened?

_____
_____
_____
_____
_____
_____
_____
_____
_____
_____
_____
_____
_____
_____

Mini-Lesson Key Points:
- Healthy relationships uplift, not drain.
- Respect, trust, and honesty are non-negotiable.

Critical Thinking Questions:
1. What are signs of an unhealthy relationship?
[Write two full paragraphs.]

_____
_____
_____
_____
_____
_____
_____
_____
_____
_____
_____

2. How can setting strong boundaries protect your well-being?
[Write two full paragraphs.]

_____

_____

_____

_____

_____

_____

_____

_____

_____

_____

_____

_____

_____

_____

Activity:
Red Flag/Green Flag Chart — List traits of healthy and unhealthy relationships.

Reflection Journal:
What will you do differently to protect your peace?
[Write two full paragraphs.]

_____
_____
_____
_____
_____
_____
_____
_____
_____
_____
_____
_____
_____
_____
_____
_____
_____
_____
_____
_____
_____
_____
_____
_____

Lesson 5: Self-Love

Objective:
I will understand that loving myself is the foundation for healthy relationships and true confidence.

Vocabulary:
- Self-Love — Regard for one's own well-being and happiness.

Do Now:
What do you love most about yourself?

_____
_____
_____
_____
_____
_____
_____
_____
_____
_____
_____
_____
_____
_____
_____

Mini-Lesson Key Points:
- Self-love isn't selfish; it's survival.
- You set the standard for how others treat you.

Critical Thinking Questions:
1. How does self-love affect the way you let others treat you?
[Write two full paragraphs.]

_____
_____
_____
_____
_____
_____
_____
_____
_____
_____

2. What are three ways you can show yourself love daily?
[Write two full paragraphs.]

_____

_____

_____

_____

_____

_____

_____

_____

_____

_____

_____

_____

_____

_____

_____

_____

Activity:
Self-Love Mirror Affirmations — Write 5 positive affirmations you can say to yourself daily.

Reflection Journal:
How will you commit to showing yourself love every day?
[Write two full paragraphs.]

_____
_____
_____
_____
_____
_____
_____
_____
_____
_____
_____
_____
_____
_____
_____
_____
_____
_____
_____
_____
_____
_____
_____
_____
_____
_____

Lesson 6: Communication Skills

Objective:
I will sharpen my verbal and non-verbal communication skills to strengthen relationships and leadership.

Vocabulary:
- Active Listening — Paying close attention to what someone is saying and responding thoughtfully.

Do Now:
Think of someone who is a great communicator. What makes them great?

_____
_____
_____
_____
_____
_____
_____
_____
_____
_____
_____
_____

Mini-Lesson Key Points:
- Communication is more listening than speaking.
- Tone, body language, and words all matter.

Critical Thinking Questions:
1. How can listening more carefully strengthen your relationships?
[Write two full paragraphs.]

_____
_____
_____
_____
_____
_____
_____
_____
_____

2. How can being a strong communicator open up more opportunities for you?
[Write two full paragraphs.]

_____
_____
_____
_____
_____
_____
_____
_____
_____
_____
_____
_____
_____
_____

Activity:
Communication Scenario Practice — Write and role-play different ways to respond thoughtfully to others.

Reflection Journal:
How will you become a better communicator starting today?
[Write two full paragraphs.]

_____

_____

_____

_____

_____

_____

_____

_____

_____

_____

_____

_____

_____

_____

_____

_____

_____

_____

_____

_____

_____

_____

_____

_____

Lesson 7: Emotional Intelligence

Objective:
I will learn the power of managing my emotions and showing empathy to others.

Vocabulary:
- Empathy — The ability to understand and share the feelings of another.

Do Now:
Describe a time when understanding someone else's feelings helped a situation.

_____
_____
_____
_____
_____
_____
_____
_____
_____
_____
_____
_____
_____
_____

Mini-Lesson Key Points:
- Emotional Intelligence (EQ) is just as important as academic intelligence.
- Self-awareness, self-control, motivation, empathy, and social skills are key pillars.

Critical Thinking Questions:
1. How does emotional intelligence make you a better leader and friend?
[Write two full paragraphs.]

_____
_____
_____
_____
_____
_____
_____
_____
_____

2. What is one area of emotional intelligence you want to grow in?
[Write two full paragraphs.]

_____
_____
_____
_____
_____
_____
_____
_____
_____
_____
_____
_____
_____
_____
_____

Activity:
EQ Strength Chart — Identify which EQ pillars are your strengths and which you want to strengthen.

Reflection Journal:
Why is leading with heart and wisdom the ultimate flex?
[Write two full paragraphs.]

_____
_____
_____
_____
_____
_____
_____
_____
_____
_____
_____
_____
_____
_____
_____
_____
_____
_____
_____
_____
_____
_____
_____
_____
_____
_____
_____
_____
_____
_____
_____
_____

Post-Reflection Survey

After completing the Knowledge of SELF curriculum, reflect on the following:

1. What is something new you learned about yourself?

2. How has your definition of success changed?

3. What parts of your identity do you embrace more now than before?

4. What are three personal goals you now feel ready to achieve?

5. How will you use what you've learned to uplift others?

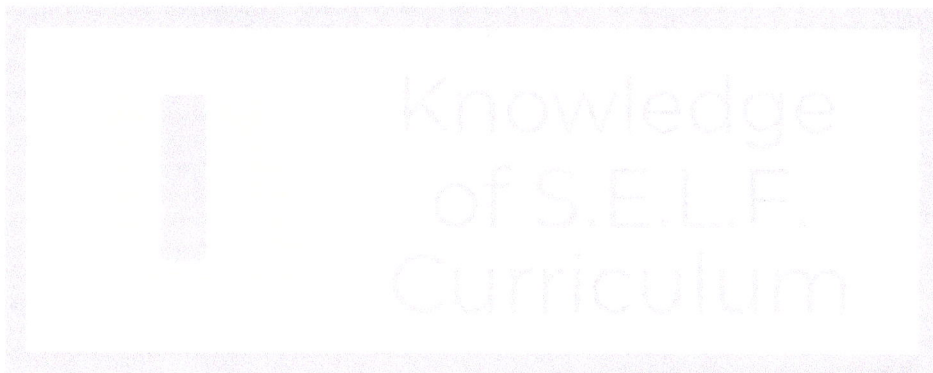